Jane Eyre

Charlotte Bronte

STUDENT PACKET

NOTE:

The trade book edition of the novel used to prepare this guide is found in the Novel Units catalog and on the Novel Units website. Using other editions may have varied page references.

Please note: We have assigned Interest Levels based on our knowledge of the themes and ideas of the books included in the Novel Units sets, however, please assess the appropriateness of this novel or trade book for the age level and maturity of your students prior to reading with them. You know your students best!

SBN 978-1-56137-463-2

To order, contact your
local school supply store, or:

Toll-Free Fax: 877.716.7272
Phone: 888.650.4224
3901 Union Blvd., Suite 155
St. Louis, MO 63115

sales@novelunits.com

novelunits.com

Name_____

Directions

Rate each of the following statements before you read the novel. Compare your ratings with a partner's, and discuss why you chose the particular ratings you did. (After you have completed the novel, discuss with your partner whether you would change any of the ratings.)

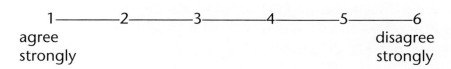

1. _____ Beauty is in the eye of the beholder.
2. _____ Opposites attract.
3. _____ It is far better to endure patiently a smart which nobody feels but yourself, than to commit a hasty action whose evil consequences will extend to all connected with you.
4. _____ Return good for evil.
5. _____ I am superstitious.
6. _____ There aren't as many class distinctions as there used to be—say 150 years ago.
7. _____ Memorizing is important to learning; students should be expected to "learn by heart" in school.
8. _____ Externals have a greater effect on children than on adults; a child's mood is more likely to reflect how bright or gloomy the environment happens to be.
9. _____ Remorse is the poison of life, so never do something you might regret later.
10. _____ It is better to have loved and lost than never to have loved at all.
11. _____ I would rather experience the highs and lows—extreme joy, bitter remorse—than to go through life on an even keel—never exhilarated, never dejected.
12. _____ Friends always forget those whom fortune forsakes.
13. _____ Love your enemies and turn the other cheek if they hurt you.

Write a brief answer to each study question as you read the novel at home or in class. Use the questions for review before group discussions and before your final exam.

Chapters 1-6:
1. Why did Jane live with Mrs. Reed and her children?
2. Who is Mr. Brocklehurst and why did he visit Mrs. Reed?
3. Who is Bessie and how does she get along with Jane?
4. Who kindly ordered a lunch of bread and cheese for the hungry girls?
5. Why did Jane decide to talk to Helen Burns?

Chapters 7-11:
6. Why did Mr. Brocklehurst order Jane to come forward in front of the other girls?
7. How did Miss Temple clear Jane's name?
8. Why did so many girls at Lowood grow ill in the spring?
9. Describe the night Helen died.
10. How long did Jane remain at Lowood?
11. How did Mrs. Fairfax treat Jane when they first met? Why was Jane surprised by that treatment?
12. What did Jane learn about her new student from Mrs. Fairfax the morning after Jane arrived?

Chapters 12-16:
13. Why was Jane discontented with her new job?
14. Who was Grace Poole and what did Jane think of her?
15. What did Mr. Rochester think of Jane's artwork and piano playing?
16. How did Adèle happen to become Mr. Rochester's ward?
17. How did Jane save Mr. Rochester's life?
18. What did Mr. Rochester and Miss Ingram have in common?

Chapters 17-19:

19. Why does Jane feel that she was being deliberately excluded from some mystery at Thornfield?
20. How did Miss Ingram treat Adèle?
21. Why didn't Jane feel that Miss Ingram was compatible with Mr. Rochester?
22. How does Miss Ingram act after returning from the fortune-teller?
23. What does the gypsy tell Jane?
24. Who is the fortune-teller? How does Jane guess?

Chapters 20-23:

25. Who is Mr. Mason and what happened to him?
26. What does Mr. Rochester ask Jane as they sit together in the orchard?
27. Why did Mrs. Reed send for Jane? Are you surprised that Jane left Mr. Rochester to go see her?
28. Mrs. Reed told Jane "I have twice done you a wrong which I regret now." What were the two wrongs?
29. On what terms were Jane and Mrs. Reed when Mrs. Reed finally died?
30. Briefly describe how and where Mr. Rochester proposed to Jane—and what ominous event occurred right afterward.

Chapters 24-26:

31. How did Mrs. Fairfax react to the news that Mr. Rochester planned to marry Jane?
32. What steps did Mr. Rochester take to prepare Jane for her wedding? How did she react to all he bought for her?
33. What happened to Jane's wedding veil while she was sleeping?
34. Who interrupted the wedding ceremony, and on what grounds?
35. Why did Mr. Rochester invite those present at the wedding to come up to his house?
36. Briefly describe the circumstances of Mr. Rochester's marriage to Bertha Mason.
37. Explain the coincidence whereby Mr. Mason learned that Mr. Rochester intended to remarry.

Chapters 27-29:
38. After revealing the truth about his marriage to Bertha, what did Mr. Rochester propose that he and Jane do?
39. When did Jane leave Thornfield and where did she go?
40. What led Jane to the Rivers' house?
41. How did St. John and his sisters treat Jane during the few days she spent recovering in their home?

Chapters 30-33:
42. What job did St. John find for Jane?
43. St. John admits that he and his sisters never met their Uncle John. Why was his death such a "misfortune" to them, then?
44. Who is Miss Oliver?
45. How did St. John discover the connection between Jane and Mr. Rochester?
46. How did Jane become rich, and what did she do with her money?
47. What was Jane delighted to discover about St. John and his sisters?

Chapters 34-38:
48. What time of year was it when Jane decided to prepare Moor House for the arrival of Diana and Mary?
49. Why did St. John ask Jane to give up German?
50. Why did Jane refuse St. John's proposal?
51. How did St. John treat Jane after her refusal?
52. What occurrence finally made Jane decide to find Mr. Rochester?
53. How did Thornfield Hall burn?
54. How was Mr. Rochester blinded?
55. Where did Jane find Mr. Rochester, and how did he react?
56. Briefly summarize how each of the following characters was faring ten years after Jane returned to Mr. Rochester: Jane, Mr. Rochester, Adèle, St. John.

Conclusions:
57. What do you think some of the themes of Jane Eyre might be?
58. What did you like best/least about this novel?

torpid (40)	diffidence (41)	antipathy (42)	subjoined (43)
ignominy (44)	influx (45)	opprobrium (47)	duplicity (50)
unwonted (52)	emulation (57)	indefatigable (77)	inanition (77)
benignant (79)	animadversion (85)	slatternly (86)	assiduity (89)
truculent (90)	cumbrous (91)		

Directions

Each member of a small group chooses several words from the list above. After examining how the words are used in context, complete word maps for each and explain your finished maps to others in your group.

Synonyms
_____
_____
_____
_____

Antonyms
_____
_____
_____
_____

Word: _____

Definition in Your Own Words: _____
_____
_____

Picture, Diagram, or Memory Device for Your Word:

Word Used in a Sentence: _____
_____
_____

chilblains (92)	moiety (93)	surtout (94)	excrescence (96)
supplication (103)	phylactery (105)	fetid (115)	soporific (120)
cuirass (130)	canzonette (134)		

Directions

Use words from the vocabulary box to complete the analogies below. Using the analogies as models, create your own analogies for five more of the vocabulary words and give them to a partner to complete.

Sample: NO is to YES as OFF is to ON

1. HEAT is to SUN STROKE as COLD is to _____.
2. VEST is to SUIT as _____ is to ARMOR.
3. 1/2 is to 1 as _____ is to WHOLE.
4. TEE SHIRT is to UNDER as _____ is to OVER
5. COFFEE is to STIMULANT as WARM MILK is to _____.
6. _____ is to _____ as _____ is to _____.
7. _____ is to _____ as _____ is to _____.
8. _____ is to _____ as _____ is to _____.
9. _____ is to _____ as _____ is to _____.
10. _____ is to _____ as _____ is to _____.

Directions

Circle the word or phrase from each list that does not belong with the others. Briefly explain how that word's meaning sets the word apart from the others. (There may be more than one defensible answer. Choose the one you can best defend.)

11. hardhat	habergeon	porte cochère	boot
12. face	character	confabulation	physiognomy
13. bureaus	armoires	dissipations	chiffonieres
14. disobedient	capricious	wayward	malevolent
15. patriot	raiment	roué	confidante
16. melancholy	sanguine	lugubrious	salubrious

exonerated (193)	sonorous (196)	predecessor (198)	contumacy (199)
protracted (199)	saturnine (202)	extirpate (204)	phlegmatic (205)
anathematized (206)	sordid (213)	acrimony (215)	sagacity (215)
meretricious (216)	propitious (230)		

Directions
Match each word below with the word in the antonym box above that means the opposite.

1._____ praised

2._____ inopportune

3._____ condemned

4._____ accord

5._____ cheerful

6._____ nurture

7._____ obedience

8._____ muted

9._____ obtuseness

10._____ brief

11._____ successor

12._____ clean

13._____ genuine

14._____ emotional

Directions
Put an "X" in the appropriate column to indicate whether the answer to the question is "yes" or "no." Briefly explain your answers in a way that demonstrates your understanding of the italicized word's meaning.

	YES	NO
Sample: Is a naiad something you would wear when swimming? *No, you would not wear a mythological water fairy (**naiad**) when swimming.*		X

1. Does an *ostler* have wings?
_____

2. Is a *philter* something you can pour?
_____

3. Could a letter be *purloined*?
_____

4. Can you keep marbles in a *mien*?
_____

5. Is an infant interested in *pecuniary* matters?
_____

6. Should you mistrust a *charlatan*?
_____

7. Can a guppy have *acumen*?
_____

8. Are you pleased when your parents *sanction* your plans?
_____

9. Could you find eggs in an *eyrie*?
_____

10. Could a beautiful woman be a *cynosure*?
_____

Directions
Each sentence below is from the novel. Using context clues, figure out the meaning of the italicized word and circle its synonym. Discuss in a small group what Jane's statements may reveal about the author's attitudes toward various groups of people (e.g., Jews, men, women, the rich, etc.) Summarize and share your insights with the whole group.

1. I shall not be your Jane Eyre any longer, but an ape in a *harlequin*'s jacket.
   jewel   spectator   tyrant   buffoon
2. Do you think I am a Jew *usurer*, seeking good investment in land?
   moneylender   chalice   victim farmer
3. May I enjoy the great good that has been *vouchsafed* to me?
   churned   accorded   shriveled   denied
4. She surveyed my whole person: in her eyes I read that they had there found no charm powerful enough to solve the *enigma*.
   mystery   discovery   calculation   appetizer
5. In his present *fractious* mood, she dared whisper no observations.
   hoary   gleeful   irritable   protective
6. "Mademoiselle is a fairy," he said, whispering mysteriously. Whereupon I told her not to mind his *badinage*.
   convening   assaulting   shouting   teasing
7. I would not exchange this one little English girl for the Grand Turk's whole *seraglio*.
   harem   school   territory   cottage
8. Instead of subsiding as night drew on, the wind seemed to *augment* its rush and deepen its roar.
   soothe   peruse   dignify   intensify
9. A *puerile* tear dimmed my eye while I looked; ashamed of it, I wiped it away.
   frosty   moist   virtuous   childish
10. I devised how I would tease you about your aristocratic tastes and your efforts to mask your *plebeian* bride in the attributes of a peeress.
    humble   naïve   majestic   virile

Directions
Fill in each blank with a word from the vocabulary box.

profligate (327)	prurience (333)	eschewed (333)	unalloyed (335)
debauchery (338)	interlocutor (340)	plover (349)	aperture (357)
chimera (360)	superfluous (371)	remuneration (373)	

1. The _____ and the seagull stood on opposite ends of the rock.

2. People who travel a lot learn not to take along _____ items.

3. He worked diligently but received little _____ for his services.

4. She is far different from the _____ your fears have made of her.

5. Light passes through the _____ on this side of the camera.

6. Magazines such as Playboy appeal to the _____ of male readers.

7. Advocates of prohibition claimed that drinking alcohol led to _____ and corrupted morals.

8. The father _____ striking the naughty child, and gave the girl a time-out instead.

9. During the questioning, the prisoner never once looked into the eyes of his _____.

10. Although he has held down a job for a year since his release from prison, she still regards him as a _____.

11. She cannot lift herself out of the depression; her sorrow is _____ and complete.

Directions
Match each word or phrase below with its synonym in the vocabulary box.

halcyon (376)	assiduous (377)	sloth (377)	zealous (378)
coruscating (380)	ignoble (381)	morass (382)	recrimination (384)
scions (385)	repine (387)	inducements (390)	hiatus (391)
hoary (395)	asp (399)	testily (404)	boon (408)
immutably (414)			

1._____ marshy ground

2._____ favor

3._____ incentives

4._____ unchangeably

5._____ tranquil

6._____ inferior

7._____ laziness

8._____ diligent

9._____ venomous snake

10._____ ardent

11._____ grumpily

12._____ glittering

13._____ gap

14._____ accusation

15._____ white with age

Directions
Add two words to each "synonym train." Words from the novel are at the beginning of each train.

1. ebullition—boiling—seething—   _____ — _____

2. fruition—fulfillment—completion—   _____ — _____

3. estrangement—alienation—removal—   _____ — _____

4. garrulous—bombastic—chatty—   _____ — _____

5. pithy—pointed—substantive—   _____ — _____

6. estimable—respected—admired—   _____ — _____

7. uncanny—ghostly—eerie—   _____ — _____

8. fetters—bonds—handcuffs—   _____ — _____

9. infallible—dependable—fail-safe—   _____ — _____

10. providence—destiny—fate—   _____ — _____

11. lucre—assets—capital—   _____ — _____

12. oblation—assistance—charity—   _____ — _____

13. propitiate—appease—assuage—   _____ — _____

Extended Metaphor

A metaphor is an implied analogy which compares one object with another, without using the words "like" or "as." ("Her eyes are sparkling emeralds.") Sometimes the comparison is pulled through an entire paragraph, poem, or work of prose. This expanded image is known as an *extended metaphor*.

I. As a whole group, reread and analyze the extended metaphors below. Discuss what two things are being compared in each extended metaphor, and identify how the comparison is stretched throughout the paragraph.

page 449: "A lover finds his mistress asleep on a mossy bank... I saw a blackened ruin."

page 399: (St. John imagines himself married to Miss Oliver, then reflects on his own reactions to that fantasy): "...I rested my temples on the breast of temptation...her promises are hollow—her offers false."

II. Now brainstorm extensions (ideas about how the items in each pair are alike). Write answers on the board.

1. Life is like a bowl of cherries. Both—
2. School is like a circus. Both—
3. Love is like war. Both—

III. Now independently brainstorm in response to the following similes:

4. The mind is like a sponge...
5. Health is like a precious gift...
6. TV is like a drug...
7. Politicians are like actors...

IV. Using one of Brontë's extended metaphors as a model, take one of the brainstormed lists (from 1 through 7 above) and develop it into a paragraph unified by an extended metaphor.

(This activity is an adaptation of a general activity described by Nancy B. Haskall on page 3 of the March 1992 NOTES PLUS published by NCTE.)

Name_____

Project: Allusions

An **allusion** is a figure of speech that makes brief reference to an historical or literary person or event. Charlotte Brontë used many allusions to the Bible, to literature, to art, to history, and to ancient myths. She used them to create mood, reveal character, and emphasize the ironies in various situations.

Most readers in Brontë's day were familiar with these references; the allusions were effective because there was a common body of knowledge shared by the writer and her readers. However, readers today may need to do some research (using a dictionary, encyclopedia, Biblical concordance, notes at the end of the novel, etc.) to understand and appreciate these allusions.

1. Write a paragraph explaining exactly to what the allusion(s) on your list refer. (Tell who, what, and when.)
2. Reread the entire section in which the allusion occurs, and write a paragraph about why Brontë used the allusion. (Tell what effect the allusion has on the reader's understanding of the situation, the character, the mood, etc.)

Examples of Allusions in *Jane Eyre*:
1. "gave me credit for being a sort of infantine Guy Fawkes" (page 58)
2. "enactment of the part of Eutychus" (page 93)
3. "I began...to feel that the Rubicon was passed" (page 98)
4. "even as the Jews of old sent their diseased to the troubled pool of Bethesda" (page 99)
5. "we feasted that evening as on nectar and ambrosia" (page 104)
6. "I forgot to prepare in imagination the Barmecide supper..." (page 106)
7. "prints...a representation of the death of Wolfe" (page 125)
8. "chests...looking...like types of the Hebrew ark" (page 137)
9. "two rows of small black doors all shut, like a corridor in some Bluebeard's castle" (page 138)
10. "the mountain will never be brought to Mahomet" (page 146)
11. "Like heath that, in the wilderness/ The wild wind whirls away" (page 147)
12. "I pass a law, unalterable as that of the Medes and Persians" (page 169)
13. "a hag like one of those who appeared to Macbeth on the heath at Forres" (page 174)
14. "as Job's leviathan broke the spear, the dart, and the habergeon" (page 174)
15. "a shore, sweet as the hills of Beulah" (page 183)
16. "Who would not be the Rizzio of so divine a Mary?" (page 207)
17. "the fiddler David..black Bothwell..James Hepburn" (pages 207-208)
18. "I dote on Corsairs" (page 208)

Directions

Lawrence Kohlberg developed a famous model of moral development which classifies people within six levels. People who operate most of the time at Level Six are considered to be the most highly developed, morally; Mahatma Gandhi exemplifies a Level Six. Here are brief descriptions of the motivations for behavior at each level:

Level One: individual acts to avoid pain or punishment
Level Two: individual acts to get a reward
Level Three: individual acts to gain approval of others
Level Four: individual acts because of belief in the law
Level Five: individual acts for the welfare of others
Level Six: individual acts according to a set of self-formulated principles that guide one's life

At which level do each of the following characters from *Jane Eyre* operate most of the time? Why do you think so?

Character	Level	Support
Jane		
Mrs. Reed		
Helen		
Miss Temple		
Mr. Brocklehurst		
Mr. Rochester		
Mrs. Fairfax		
Adèle		
St. John		

Name_____

Directions

a. **Pre-Writing:** In a small group, complete the Venn diagram by listing words and phrases that describe each character below that character's name. Descriptors that apply to both Mr. Rochester and St. John should go in the overlapping area.

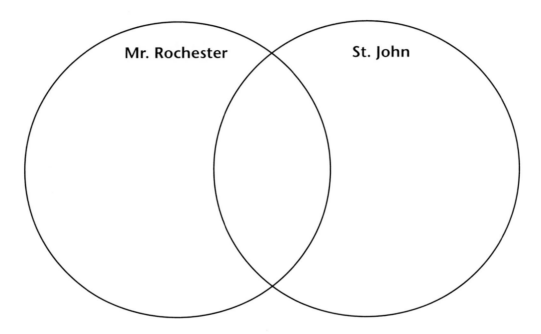

Bertha

b. **Mid-Writing:** On your own, write an essay in which you compare and contrast the characters of Mr. Rochester and St. John. Use some of the following transitional phrases to connect your ideas:

also, alike, both, common, equally, in the same way, just as/so, likewise, same, too, similar, similarly, although, but differ, different, however, in contrast, on the other hand, unlike, whereas, while.

Incorporate details from the diagram above and from the previous activity (Kohlberg's levels) to develop and support your statements about each character.

c. **Post-Writing:** Share your essay with members of your group. Ask fof comments, particularly on focus (whether you stuck to the topic) and support (whether you provided enough reasons for your statements).

Name_____

Directions

A symbol is a word, character, object, or happening that stands for something else of deeper or wider meaning. For example, the dove is often a symbol of peace. Symbolism is often developed through imagery, language that appeals to the senses.

Pre-Writing: In a small group...

a. Generate as many examples of symbols—both visual and verbal—as you can.

b. Charlotte Brontë introduces many symbols throughout *Jane Eyre*. Character names, for example, are often more than just arbitrary designations. The sound and meaning of a character's name often tells you something about that character. Discuss why each of the following names is particularly fitting. Jot down your ideas about what the symbolic significance of each name might be:

Name	Sound Suggests	Matches Character Because
Jane EYRE		
Mr. BROCKLEHURST		
Miss TEMPLE		
the REED family		
the RIVERS family		
THORNFIELD Hall		

On Your Own

When the narrator refers repeatedly to a particular event, the repetition is often a clue to symbolism. For example, the splitting of the horse chestnut is mentioned several times. How is the splitting of the tree like the relationship between Jane and Mr. Rochester?

Write a paragraph explaining the symbolic significance of one of the character names or the splitting of the tree. Explain the parallels between the name or event and the lives of the characters. Draw a conclusion about what the author is trying to emphasize by using that particular symbol.

Post-Writing

Staple a blank page to your composition and form a "round-robin" editing group. Each person comments on a composition, then passes it to the left.

Directions

Brontë gives little description of the home Jane and Mr. Rochester share. For this activity, you will write a description of their Ferndean home as you imagine it, on the morning after their first child is born.

Pre-Writing

1. Feel free to consult books on architecture and furnishings of the period in which the story is set to stimulate your imagination.
2. With a partner, discuss and jot down ideas about what you already know of Ferndean from the novel. In what sort of setting is it located? How is it constructed?
3. Imagine the exterior of the house. Is it bathed in moonlight? bright daylight? How does the exterior appear? Is there a garden near the house?
4. Visualize the interior of the house. Where are Mr. Rochester and Jane in your "picture"? How much evidence would you see of Mr. Rochester's "pre-Jane" life? Speculate about the impact Jane would have on the home. What furnishings would there probably be? What pictures on the walls? What books on the shelves? What degree of orderliness? How does the room make you feel?

Mid-Writing

Individually, write a description of Ferndean. Use transitional words from the following list to help your reader "see" where things lie in relation to each other:

above, on top of, upon, over, left, right below, on the bottom of, beneath, under, east, west, north, south, around, surrounding, in back (front) of, behind, between, among, opposite, in the middle of, in the center of, beside, next to.

Post-Writing

Read your description to others who have read the novel. Have them comment on how vividly they were able to "see" what you describe; they might even make a sketch based on your description. Also ask for comments on how consistent listeners feel your interpretation of Ferndean is with details the author has provided about her characters and settings throughout the novel.

Charlotte Brontë was a meticulous writer who selected each word carefully. She deliberately included several "vulgarisms" of the day (e.g., "optics" for "eyes"). She had a sharp ear for dialects—variations in spoken English among speakers of different classes and from different parts of England.

Directions
1. "Translate" each of the passages below in which into standard English for Hannah.
2. Rewrite one of the passages in another dialect of your choice.

    a. page 359: "Well, for sure case, I knawn't how they can understand t'one t'other: and if either o'ye went there, ye could tell what they said, I guess?"

    b. page 359: "Varry like: but give ower studying; ye've done enough for tonight."

    c. pages 359-360: "Ah, childer! 'it fair troubles me to go into yond' room no."

    d. page 360: "He hadn't time, bairn: he was gone in a minute, was your father. He had been a bit ailing like the day before, but naught to signify; and when Mr. St. John asked if he would like either of you to be sent for, he fair laughed at him."

    e. page 369: "'No more I ought,' said she: 'Mr. St. John tells me so, too; and I see I wor wrang—but I've clear a different notion on you now to what I had. You look a raight down dacent little crater.'"

Rewrite of letter _____:

Name_____

Directions

Suppose that you are "Gabby"—a syndicated advice columnist. You receive this letter:

Dear *Gabby*,

I read your column every day and enjoy it a great deal. I never thought in a million years that I would be one of those writing to you for advice—I'm usually the one people turn to with their problems. I'm in a real pickle now, though, and I have nowhere else to turn, so here goes. The man I'm in love with also happens to be my boss—a man twice my age—but that isn't the problem. (I can handle the fact that he's my employer and that he's so much older, even if others can't.) The problem is that he's married. We were engaged to be married—made it to the altar, in fact. Then— WHAM—just like in the movies, someone stopped the ceremony with the news that my husband-shortly-to-be had a wife! To make a long story short, soon after meeting the wife—a violent, psychotic woman—I left the guy. Now I've met someone else— handsome, intelligent, refined—and he has asked me to marry him and go off to India to do missionary work with him. There's just one hitch: I don't love him and he doesn't love me. I'm still in love with that would-be bigamist. What should I do?
Plain Jane

In a small group, brainstorm possible actions Jane might take and weigh the pros and cons of each. (A chart for organizing your ideas is shown below.) Then write a letter of advice to Jane, using evidence from the completed chart.

Choice #1:			Choice #2:	
_____			_____	
_____			_____	
Pros	**Cons**		**Pros**	**Cons**
		What should Jane do?		

Choice #3: _____
Pros:

Cons:

Name_____

In literature and drama, the plot often is carried along by the causes and effects of decisions made by the characters. Had the characters made an alternate decision—or had a particular coincidence not occurred—the plot would have turned in a different direction. Even small decisions—or coincidences—can have a great impact on later events.

Directions

In a small group discussion, discuss two coincidences that occur in the story: (a) the one leading to Jane's discovery that St. John and his sisters are her cousins, and (b) the one leading to Jane's uncle's discovery that his niece is preparing to marry a man who is already married. Talk about the cause-effect chain that leads to each discovery, and summarize the causes and effects below.

a:

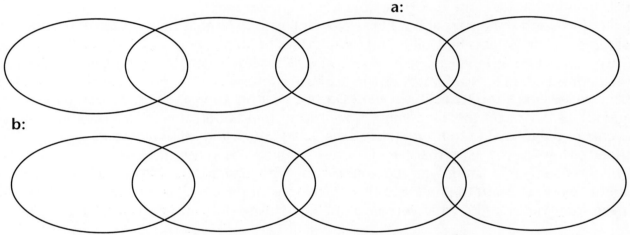

b:

Speculate about how the story would have been different without these coincidental events. For instance—

Jane finds shelter with a farmer and works as a dairymaid.	Plot Changes →	

Jane's uncle hires a lawyer who knows nothing about Mr. Rochester's past.	Plot Changes →	

Name_____

In the novel, we do not see how Mr. Rochester reacts when he discovers that Jane has left (following the aborted wedding ceremony). In this exercise, you will write a monologue for Mr. Rochester that reveals what he thinks and feels when he finds that Jane is gone.

Pre-Writing

Teacher or group leader:
"Take a few minutes to relax and imagine the events of the previous day. Recreate the wedding scene. Picture the interior of the church. Who is there? What is the lighting like? Walk through the scene with the strangers as they walk up to Jane and Mr. Rochester. Can you hear what they say? Notice the angry expression on Mr. Rochester's face...follow him as he leads you to the room where Bertha is kept. Can you see how tall she is? What does she do? How does Mr. Rochester react? Can you hear what he is telling Jane and the others about her?...Now follow him later as he goes to sit in front of Jane's room. What is he waiting for? What does he think about as he waits? Notice their expressions as Jane wakens and sees him. Where do they go to talk? Can you hear their conversation?...Now watch as Mr. Rochester throws himself on the sofa and sobs. Do you see Jane kneel to kiss his cheek? Do you hear her tone as she says "Farewell" and leaves him?...Let the happenings flow in your mind until you realize how the events of the following morning take shape....Put yourself in Mr. Rochester's shoes....How do you learn that Jane is gone—not just late in rising? How do you react? How do you feel? What do you remember about the previous day? What do you think about? Now return to the here and now, pick up your pen, and take a few minutes to make some notes about what you have just seen, heard, felt, and thought about."

Assignments

1. Do an oral improvisation of the scene. Speak your thoughts aloud, as in a stage soliloquy. (You might find it helpful to tape the improvisation and play it back for discussion.)
2. Transcribe your improvisation onto paper. As you write, think about Mr. Rochester's way of thinking, his speech patterns, his feelings toward Jane, and the way he has acted in the past when angered or disappointed.
3. Perform the monologue, complete with gestures, for others who have read the novel. Have them comment on how believable your monologue sounds. Are the thoughts themselves—and the words which you have chosen to convey them— consistent with Mr. Rochester as we know him from the novel? Is that the way you would expect Mr. Rochester to act?

© Novel Units, Inc.

24

Name_____

Directions

Answer each question below in a sentence or two. Use separate paper.

1. Why did Jane live with Mrs. Reed as a child?
2. Why did Mrs. Reed send Jane away to Lowood?
3. Why was Jane miserable after Mr. Brocklehurst visited Lowood?
4. Who was Miss Temple and how did Jane feel about her?
5. Who was Helen and what caused her death?
6. During Bessie's visit to Lowood, what did Jane learn about her Uncle John?
7. Why did Jane decide to leave her teaching job at Lowood?
8. Why did Mrs. Fairfax invite Jane to Thornfield?
9. How did Jane assist Mr. Rochester the first time she met him?
10. How did Jane assist Mr. Rochester the night she discovered the fire?

Write the word or phrase that properly completes each statement.

11. Soon after meeting Jane, Mr. Rochester complimented her on her talent at _____.

12. Mr. Rochester sent Mrs. Fairfax a letter directing her to prepare the house because he was planning _____.

13. Mr. Rochester disguised himself as a _____ and asked to see only the young female guests.

14. Despite the disguise, Jane recognized Mr. Rochester when she saw his _____.

15. Blanche Ingram seemed _____ after talking with the gypsy.

16. Jane suspected that _____ was responsible for setting the fire that could have killed Mr. Rochester.

17. Mr. Rochester told Jane that he experienced great jealousy when he discovered _____'s mother with another man.

18. Jane noticed that whenever Grace Poole left the kitchen, she usually had a(n) _____ in her hand.

19. Jane told Mr. Rochester that it was a pity that Adèle didn't _____ him more; if she had, perhaps he wouldn't find her so annoying.

20. At Mr. Rochester's party, Jane was surprised and moved to find that Mr. Rochester had a fine, rich _____.

Name_____

True-False: Write "T" if the statement is true. Write "F" if the statement is false.

_____ 1. Jane lived with Mrs. Reed because she had promised her husband to take care of his sister's orphaned daughter.

_____ 2. Mrs. Reed sent Jane away to Lowood because she realized that Jane was a very bright girl who would do well in a good school.

_____ 3. Jane was miserable after Mr. Brocklehurst visited Lowood because he informed everyone that she was a bad girl.

_____ 4. Miss Temple was a harsh teacher at Lowood whom Jane particularly detested.

_____ 5. Jane's best friend, Helen, died as a result of the beating she received from one of her teachers.

_____ 6. After her student days at Lowood, Jane stayed on at Lowood as a teacher.

_____ 7. Jane learned from Bessie that her own Uncle John had tried to locate her seven years before.

_____ 8. Jane decided to leave Lowood because she could no longer stand the constant hunger and cold.

_____ 9. Jane accepted a post as governess at Thornfield.

_____ 10. The first time Jane met Mr. Rochester, she helped him by bandaging a snakebite on his arm.

_____ 11. Mr. Rochester complimented Jane on her talented piano playing.

_____ 12. Mr. Rochester sent Mrs. Fairfax a letter directing her to prepare the house because he was planning to sell it.

_____ 13. Mr. Rochester disguised himself as a gypsy and asked to see only the young female guests.

_____ 14. Despite the disguise, Jane recognized Mr. Rochester because of his shoes.

_____ 15. Mr. Rochester seemed happy to learn that Mr. Mason had come to see him.

_____ 16. Jane suspected that Mr. Rochester himself had set fire to his room.

_____ 17. Mr. Rochester told Jane that he felt jealous when he discovered Adèle's mother with another man.

_____ 18. Jane noticed that whenever Grace Poole left the kitchen, she usually had an alcoholic drink in her hand.

_____ 19. Jane told Mr. Rochester that it was a pity that Adèle didn't resemble him more, for if she had he might have liked her more.

_____ 20. At Mr. Rochester's party, Jane was surprised and moved to find that Mr. Rochester had a fine, rich singing voice.

Identification

Find a character on the right who matches the description on the left. Write the number of the character next to the matching letter. Each character is to be used only once.

1. Jane Eyre
2. Mrs. Reed
3. Georgiana Reed
4. Eliza Reed
5. John Reed
6. Mr. Lloyd
7. Mr. Brocklehurst
8. Miss Temple

9. Mrs. Fairfax
10. Mr. Rochester
11. Adèle
12. Celine Varens
13. Blanche Ingram
14. Grace Poole
15. Bertha
16. Mr. Mason

17. Jane's Uncle John
18. St. John Rivers
19. Diana Rivers
20. Mary Rivers
21. Miss Oliver
22. Hannah
23. Bessie

_____ A. He decided that Jane's nerves were not in a good state and asked if she would like to go to school

_____ B. She did not resemble Mr. Rochester but might have been his illegitimate daughter.

_____ C. She was a pious and gentle teacher who engaged Helen in complex scholarly discussions.

_____ D. She was an attractive woman who accepted someone else when St. John failed to propose to her.

_____ E. a "black marble" Evangelical clergyman who brings the bogy of hell-fire religion into Jane's life

_____ F. the tall, dark, supercilious woman who saw herself as the future Mrs. Rochester until learning about his finances

_____ G. She never happened to see her son abusing or teasing Jane.

_____ H. the Rivers sister who, along with Jane, tended to let her sister lead in conversation

_____ I. a flamboyant mother who taught her daughter to sing and dance

_____ J. His avaricious father and brother arranged his marriage to a beautiful Creole woman.

_____ K. As an adult, she loved being the center of attention and would have eloped if her jealous sister hadn't snitched.

_____ L. He never made up with his brother and sister-in-law, named Rivers, after getting with them into a business deal that turned sour.

_____ M. He tortured animals and young Jane as a child, and lived a dissolute and short adult life.

____ N. Jane admired the learning and leadership qualities of this woman, probably modeled after Charlotte Brontë's sister.

____ O. This protagonist and narrator passes from childhood through adulthood within the covers of the novel.

____ P. Jane assumed at first that this good woman was Adèle's mother.

____ Q. Mr. Rochester had no idea that there was a history of madness in this woman's family.

____ R. a high-minded cleric who prided himself on subduing his impulses for the service of God

____ S. Bertha's handsome brother who showed up with a lawyer to stop Mr. Rochester's wedding to Jane

____ T. Bertha sometimes slipped away from her when she had been drinking.

____ U. the aloof, less pretty Reed sister who eventually became a spinster and found a substitute for life in High Anglicanism

____ V. She exclaimed about what a "lady" Jane had turned out to be.

____ W. She turned Jane away from Moor House because she felt it her duty to protect the Rivers family from "common beggars."

Multiple Choice: Indicate the number of the BEST response.

____ 1. The settings in the novel parallel the phases in Jane's development: early childhood, girlhood, adolescence, maturity, fulfillment in marriage. Which was the setting of Jane's girlhood?
(1) Gateshead   (3) Thornfield
(2) Lowood   (4) Marsh End

____ 2. Eliza, St. John, and Mr. Brocklehurst are alike in what way?
(1) All sermonize about the right way for others to live, while behaving in a contrary way.
(2) All are wealthy individuals who are guided by religious values rather than materialism.
(3) All claim to be religious people, but show little love for the people near them.
(4) All accuse Jane of being a deceitful liar while it is they who use deceit and lies.

____ 3. The chapter of the novel detailing the day before the planned wedding is characterized by what tone?
(1) sober   (3) bitter
(2) ominous   (4) joyous

____ 4. If Jane had decided to do as Helen Burns would have done after the wedding was called off, she might well have
   (1) gone away with Mr. Rochester to the Continent
   (2) allowed herself to die of want and cold
   (3) refused to forgive Mr. Rochester for his betrayal
   (4) left Thornfield and pleaded for food and shelter

____ 5. Jane loses her spontaneity in the presence of _____, who is the antithesis of _____.

(1) St. John, Mr. Rochester	(3) Diana, Georgiana
(2) Mr. Rochester, St. John	(4) Miss Ingram, Miss Oliver

____ 6. Jane's escape from St. John to Mr. Rochester is the reverse of her flight from _____; this time she has few doubts about leaving the man behind.

(1) Gateshead	(3) Thornfield
(2) Lowood	(4) Ferndean

____ 7. The "tragic, preternatural" laughter that Jane hears at Thornfield is that of

(1) Mr. Rochester	(3) Grace Poole
(2) Adèle	(4) Bertha

____ 8. Charlotte Brontë's heroine, Jane, demands the freedom of self-determination; perhaps it is no mistake that Jane's last name suggests the word for a mighty eagle's lofty nest, an _____

(1) aerugo	(3) eyrie
(2) aero	(4) erring

____ 9. Moor House is the antithesis of Gateshead; the "broken Reeds are replaced by the _____ of life" when Jane finds fortune and family at Moor House.

(1) Bitternuts	(3) Burns
(2) Temples	(4) Rivers

____ 10. Mrs. Reed's behavior when dying is most like that of
   (1) a condemned prisoner who begs for mercy
   (2) a hospital patient who requests that her family stay away to spare them pain
   (3) an irritable traveler who confesses to hiding undeclared goods before passing through customs
   (4) an animal that goes into the woods to die alone

_____ 11. If Mrs. Reed had told Jane about the letter from John Eyre when it first arrived, Jane probably would
    (1) have gone to Madeira to live with her uncle
    (2) never have gone to Lowood
    (3) have married St. John
    (4) never have left Mr. Rochester

_____ 12. If Jane hadn't happened to knock on the door at Marsh End, she probably never would have discovered that
    (1) John Reed had died
    (2) she had living cousins
    (3) Mr. Rochester was married
    (4) Bertha was mad

_____ 13. If Mr. Mason hadn't happened to visit Madeira, Jane's uncle would never have
    (1) written to Mrs. Reed about Jane
    (2) died so young
    (3) had the wedding called off
    (4) cut the Rivers out of his will

_____ 14. Jane probably fainted in the red room because she was
    (1) acting in order to get her aunt to let her out
    (2) lonely without her doll
    (3) terrified that her uncle's ghost would be there
    (4) suffering from a concussion

_____ 15. When Mr. Brocklehurst gave Jane a book to read, it was an act of
    (1) futility because she could not read yet
    (2) kindness because she was rarely given her own books
    (3) sympathy because the book was about loneliness
    (4) coldness because the book was meant to frighten her

_____ 16. Which of the following is NOT an example of supernatural elements in the novel?
    (1) Mr. Rochester's speculation about why he fell from his horse
    (2) the figure who told Jane to "flee temptation" when Jane learned of Mr. Rochester's wife
    (3) the numerous deaths of girls at Lowood
    (4) the voice Jane heard calling her back to Mr. Rochester

____ 17. The reason Miss Temple wrote to Mr. Lloyd was to find out if Jane was telling the truth about
(1) the hardships she suffered while living at Gateshead
(2) her aunt's promise to her uncle
(3) fainting in the red room
(4) being the daughter of a clergyman

____ 18. Jane advertised her services as governess because
(1) she lost her teaching job at Lowood
(2) she was emotionally and physically drained by Lowood
(3) she was hoping to expand her marital prospects
(4) she wanted to experience more of the world

____ 19. When Jane first met St. John's sisters, they were wearing mourning clothes because _____ had just died.
(1) their elder brother   (3) their uncle
(2) their father   (4) their mother

____ 20. Remembering her conversation with Mr. Lloyd, Jane reflects, "No, I was not heroic enough to purchase liberty at the price of caste." As a child, Jane
(1) was unwilling to live with poor relatives
(2) didn't have enough money to find her relatives
(3) believed that the poor were as worthy as the rich
(4) preferred being poor to being enslaved

____ 21. Jane's parents died of the same disease as
(1) Helen   (3) Mr. Rochester's elder brother
(2) many girls at Lowood   (4) Uncle John Eyre

____ 22. When Mr. Brocklehurst asked Jane what she must do to avoid falling into the pit and burning in hell, her response—"I must keep in good health, and not die"—revealed her
(1) innocence and naivete   (3) ignorance of Scripture
(2) capacity for sarcasm   (4) sense of humor

_____ 23. When Helen tells Jane, "It is far better to endure patiently a smart which nobody feels but yourself, than to commit a hasty action whose evil consequences will extend to all connected with you," she means
   (1) stop sitting around feeling sorry for yourself and do something
   (2) realize that you are not the only one who feels that way
   (3) speak up so others will not have to go through the same thing
   (4) don't complain or else someone else will get hurt

_____ 24. After leaving Mr. Rochester, Jane sought assistance by knocking on her cousins' door. Which of the following devices is the author using here?
   (1) coincidence   (3) hyperbole
   (2) personification   (4) symbolism

_____ 25. Which of the following is NOT an example of flashback?
   (1) There was no possibility of taking a walk that day.
   (2) My first quarter at Lowood seemed an age.
   (3) Merry days were these at Thornfield Hall.
   (4) I have now been married ten years.

_____ 26. What atmosphere is created by the following description: "I lingered in the long passage to which this led...narrow, low, and dim...and looking like a corridor in some Bluebeard's castle."
   (1) tranquil and peaceful   (3) gloomy and threatening
   (2) cheerful and gay   (4) shifting and unpredictable

_____ 27. What tone do you imagine Mr. Rochester to use when he tells Adèle, "Yes, there is your 'boite' at last: take it into a corner, you genuine daughter of Paris, and amuse yourself with disembowelling it..."
   (1) warm, affectionate   (3) wry, ironic
   (2) bitter, disgusted   (4) polite, gracious

_____ 28. What is ironic about Lady Ingram's comment that Jane should not be asked to join the others in playing charades as "she looks too stupid for any game of the sort"?
   (1) Jane is more intelligent than Lady Ingram.
   (2) Lady Ingram herself is too stupid to play.
   (3) Jane has no desire to play.
   (4) Lady Ingram's daughter is too stupid to play.

____ 29. While talking about Bertha, Mr. Rochester told Jane, "Your mind is my treasure, and if it were broken, it would be my treasure still." He meant:
(1) He valued Jane for her mind, not her body.
(2) If he couldn't have Jane, no one could.
(3) If Jane left, he would always keep memories of her.
(4) If she went mad, he would still love her.

____ 30. The ending of the novel is effective because it
(1) leaves the reader on a final happy note as Jane describes her marital happiness in the last lines
(2) surprises the reader by raising an unanswered question about what really happened to Mr. Rochester's wife
(3) provides a sense of closure by finally answering a question about Mr. Rochester's affair with Celine
(4) underlines Charlotte Brontë's dislike of dogmatic religion by leaving the reader with news of St. John's impending death

I. Analysis

Directions
Select A or B and indicate the letter of the question you decide to answer.

Choose the alternative that best represents your opinion. Explain the reasons for your choice in a short paragraph on a separate sheet of paper. Cite evidence from the book to support your opinion.

    A. By leaving Mr. Rochester when she learned about his wife, Jane revealed her
        (1) personal integrity
        (2) artificially trained conscience
        (3) other

    B. If Jane were married to Mr. Rochester today, which of the following do you think she would most likely choose to be?
        (1) homemaker
        (2) book illustrator
        (3) NOW president
        (4) teacher at a private school
        (5) other _____

II. Critical and Creative Thinking

Select C or D.

    C. You are Jane Eyre and you have just discovered that the Rivers siblings are your cousins. Write an entry in your journal. Mention some of your thoughts and feelings about Diana, Mary and St. John. Contrast them with the three individuals with whom you grew up—Georgiana, Eliza, and John Reed.

    D. Write an essay on the symbolic significance of the chestnut tree in Jane Eyre. Explain what happens to the tree, and explore the deeper meaning that event might have. Be sure to include a thesis and to defend that thesis with plenty of evidence from the story.

Identification

Find a character on the right who matches the description on the left. Write the number of the character next to the matching letter. Each character is to be used only once.

1. Jane Eyre	9. Mrs. Fairfax	17. Jane's Uncle John
2. Mrs. Reed	10. Mr. Rochester	18. St. John Rivers
3. Georgiana Reed	11. Adèle	19. Diana
4. Eliza	12. Celine Varens	20. Mary
5. John Reed	13. Blanche Ingram	21. Miss Oliver
6. Mr. Lloyd	14. Grace Poole	22. Bessie
7. Mr. Brocklehurst	15. Bertha Mason	23. Hannah
8. Miss Temple	16. Mr. Mason	

_____ A. the sympathetic apothecary who sees Jane after she faints in the red room

_____ B. the little girl Jane is hired to teach

_____ C. a kind teacher at Lowood

_____ D. the lovely woman who has her eye on St. John

_____ E. the grim director of Lowood

_____ F. the lovely woman who has her eye on Mr. Rochester

_____ G. Jane's detested guardian, her aunt-by-marriage

_____ H. Diana's and St. John's sister

_____ I. Adèle's mother and Mr. Rochester's mistress

_____ J. the master of Thornfield Hall

_____ K. the pretty, spoiled Reed sister with the golden hair

_____ L. the brother of Jane's father, he left her his money

_____ M. Mrs. Reed's spoiled, cruel son

_____ N. the handsome Rivers daughter who enjoyed teaching Jane German

_____ O. the narrator of the novel

_____ P. Mr. Rochester's relative and kindly manager of his home

_____ Q. Mr. Rochester's mad wife

_____ R. the cold minister who proposed to Jane

_____ S. Mr. Rochester's brother-in-law

_____ T. Mr. Rochester hired her to take care of Bertha

_____ U. the Reed sister who ends up in a convent

_____ V. the Rivers' servant who turned Jane away at first

_____ W. the employee of Mrs. Reed's who sometimes told Jane stories

Directions
Indicate the number of the BEST response.

_____ 1. Mrs. Reed promised _____ that she would raise Jane Eyre.
(1) Jane's mother, Mrs. Reed's sister
(2) Jane's father, Mr. Reed's brother
(3) Jane's aunt, Mrs. Reed's sister
(4) Jane's uncle, Mrs. Reed's husband

_____ 2. Which of the following words best describes what Mrs. Reed felt for Jane Eyre?
(1) respect   (3) affection
(2) envy   (4) dislike

_____ 3. Jane was locked in the red room after
(1) telling Mrs. Reed she wanted to go to school
(2) defending herself against an attack by John Reed
(3) stealing a valuable book from Mrs. Reed's library
(4) lying to Mr. Brocklehurst about her prayers

_____ 4. Helen Burns expressed her belief that you should
(1) suffer silently   (3) keep your body fit
(2) give up sweets   (4) defend yourself

_____ 5. Which of the following best describes Jane's feelings about Helen?
(1) Jane wanted to be just like Helen.
(2) Jane felt that Helen was like her twin.
(3) Jane admired Helen.
(4) Jane envied Helen's rebelliousness.

_____ 6. Most of the girls at Lowood were
(1) preparing to be nuns   (3) children from wealthy families
(2) daughters of ministers   (4) orphans

_____ 7. Miss Temple cleared Jane's name after everyone at school heard Mr. Brocklehurst accuse her of being a
(1) liar   (3) thief
(2) murderer   (4) bully

_____ 8. Conditions at Lowood improved only after
     (1) Mr. Brocklehurst's daughters arrived there
     (2) Mr. Brocklehurst listened to Jane's plea
     (3) many girls died of typhus
     (4) Miss Temple took over

_____ 9. Jane Eyre left Lowood when
     (1) Helen died   (3) Miss Temple married
     (2) Mrs. Reed called her home (4) she finished her studies at age 16

_____ 10. Bessie visited Jane at Lowood and told her that seven years earlier
     (1) John had died   (3) Jane's uncle had come looking for her
     (2) Mrs. Reed had died   (4) Georgiana had eloped

_____ 11. After meeting Mrs. Fairfax, Jane was
     (1) pleased that the good woman was not another Mrs. Reed
     (2) put off by Mrs. Fairfax's coldness and stiffness
     (3) irritated to learn that Mrs. Fairfax was a servant, not her employer
     (4) curious to know why Mrs. Fairfax had hired her

_____ 12. Jane soon discovered that her pupil, Adèle___
     (1) was a disobedient brat   (3) liked to sing and dance
     (2) was a diligent student   (4) liked to annoy Jane

_____ 13. Jane met Mr. Rochester
     (1) when he picked her up at the station
     (2) when she first walked up the lane to Thornfield
     (3) after he fell off his horse
     (4) after she tripped over his dog

_____ 14. When Mr. Rochester asked Jane if she considered him handsome, she told him
     (1) no   (3) somewhat
     (2) yes   (4) she couldn't say

_____ 15. Jane suspected at first that the strange laughter and the fire could both be traced to
     (1) Grace Poole   (3) Mrs. Fairfax
     (2) Bertha Mason   (4) Adèle's mother

____ 16. The way Jane felt as she watched Mr. Rochester with Miss Ingram can best be compared to the way you feel when
  (1) you are forced to watch a film showing a bloody accident
  (2) you choose to watch your favorite TV comedy
  (3) you find yourself pressing a bruise on your arm
  (4) you cut your hand while slicing a bagel

____ 17. While disguised as a gypsy, Mr. Rochester
  (1) avoided discovery by Mr. Mason
  (2) kissed Jane
  (3) told Blanche that Mr. Rochester wasn't a great catch
  (4) told Jane that Mr. Rochester would be a great catch

____ 18. Mr. Mason recognized the woman who attacked him because
  (1) he had read a description of her   (3) he had seen a picture of her
  (2) she was his patient   (4) she was his sister

____ 19. When she grew ill, Mrs. Reed sent for Jane in order to
  (1) apologize to Jane
  (2) die with a clean conscience
  (3) ask Jane to take care of her
  (4) tell her one last time how much she hated her

____ 20. John Eyre wrote a letter to Mrs. Reed in which he told of his desire to
  (1) go to India   (3) hire Jane
  (2) adopt Jane   (4) become a wine merchant

____ 21. Which of the following best describes Mrs. Fairfax's reaction when she learned that Jane planned to marry Mr. Rochester?
  (1) Whooppppeeeeee!   (3) Are you sure you know what you're doing?
  (2) How could you?!   (4) Dream on!

____ 22. Jane did not marry Mr. Rochester at the church as planned because
  (1) she did not like the way he was trying to change her
  (2) Mr. Rochester was charged with already having a wife
  (3) she convinced him that his love for her would fade
  (4) he convinced her that they should elope to Europe

____ 23. After leaving Thornfield, Jane might have died in the cold if she had not been taken in by
  (1) Hannah   (3) Miss Oliver
  (2) St. John   (4) Mrs. Fairfax

_____ 24. Jane decided to share her inheritance from Uncle John with St. John and his sisters because they
  (1) promised to help her use it to improve Lowood
  (2) convinced her that wealth would corrupt her
  (3) needed the money to start a school for girls
  (4) deserved it since they were also related to Uncle John

_____ 25. Jane did not marry St. John mainly because
  (1) he did not ask her
  (2) he did not love her
  (3) she had vowed never to marry
  (4) she had promised to return to Mr. Rochester

_____ 26. It was a coincidence that Jane, cold and hungry, happened to knock on the door of
  (1) Helen's relatives   (3) Bertha Mason's relatives
  (2) Mr. Rochester's relatives (4) her own relatives

_____ 27. It was a coincidence that Mr. Mason, while visiting Madeira, happened to meet the uncle of
  (1) the woman who was about to marry his brother-in-law
  (2) the woman who had attacked him at Thornfield Hall
  (3) the woman who had raised Jane Eyre
  (4) the woman who had had a child by Mr. Rochester

_____ 28. St. John did not marry Miss Oliver mainly because
  (1) he did not love her
  (2) she did not love him
  (3) he did not know she loved him
  (4) she would not have made a good missionary

_____ 29. Jane decided to return to Mr. Rochester after
  (1) learning that he had been blinded (3) receiving a letter from him
  (2) Mrs. Fairfax begged her to return (4) hearing his voice call to her

_____ 30. Mr. Rochester was blinded
  (1) in a fire set by his mad wife
  (2) by cataracts that worsened with aging
  (3) by grief over losing Jane
  (4) by his own hand

I. Analysis

Directions

Select A or B and write a paragraph with complete sentences and at least three clearly explained examples or reasons. Indicate the letter of the question you answer.

A. Explain why Jane finally decides she must return to Mr. Rochester.

B. Describe some of the dreams Jane has. Explain what these dreams have to do with the problems Jane faces.

II. Critical/Creative Thinking

Directions

Select C or D.

C. You are Jane. Write a letter to Bessie describing your new job as governess and your new employer, Mr. Rochester.

D. Imagine that Jane returns to Mr. Rochester—and finds that his wife Bertha is still living. Write a scene telling how Jane and Mr. Rochester greet each other and showing what they decide to do. You may use drama form if you wish.

Answer Key

Activity #1: Students' answers will vary.

Answers to Study Questions:
1. Mrs. Reed's husband, Jane's uncle, made his wife promise to take care of orphaned Jane after he died.
2. The head of Lowood School, he came to talk to Mrs. Reed about enrolling Jane.
3. A servant, Bessie treats Jane more kindly than anyone else in the household.
4. Miss Temple
5. She hoped to borrow the book Helen was reading.
6. Jane broke her slate, and this reminded Brocklehurst of the lies Mrs. Reed had told him, about Jane—which he related to the entire student body and staff.
7. She wrote to Mr. Lloyd, then announced she had found Brocklehurst's claims false.
8. typhus
9. Jane went to see her, and was found curled up with Helen's dead body the next morning.
10. 8 years
11. She was very friendly and not at all bossy; Jane thought she was the lady of the house.
12. Adèle is the ward of Mr. Rochester, who owns Thornfield.
13. She found "woman's work" rather boring, and wanted to use her mind and her abilities.
14. Grace, a servant who did most of the sewing and kept a very low profile, seemed strange to Jane, especially when she heard the insane laughter attributed to her.
15. He was very impressed.
16. She is possibly his illegitimate daughter by Celine Varens, his French mistress, who abandoned the little girl to his care.
17. She woke to find his bed on fire and doused the flames.
18. Very little other than the same social class.
19. The mysterious upper room and the odd laughter make her wonder what's being hidden.
20. She looked down on her, and found her a bother.
21. She could tell Mr. Rochester wasn't "charmed" by Blanche.
22. She acted put-out, and stared at a book without reading it.
23. The gypsy tells Jane she was within reach of happiness, if only she would stretch out her hand to touch it.
24. Mr. Rochester; She sees his ring.
25. A visitor from the West Indies, he is bitten, apparently by Grace Poole.
26. to sit up with him the night before he marries Blanche
27. She is on her deathbed.
28. The first was that she broke her promise to her husband to bring up Jane as one of her own children; the second was that when Jane's Uncle John wrote that he wanted to adopt her, Mrs. Reed told him Jane was dead.
29. They remained unreconciled, although Jane was quite willing to forgive.
30. Under the horse-chestnut tree, Mr. Rochester spoke of his upcoming marriage—then told Jane she was the one he planned to marry. Later, lightning split the tree in half.
31. She was dubious and protective of Jane.
32. He wanted to buy her fancy clothes and accessories, but Jane felt he was trying to make her into something she wasn't.

---

33. Someone or something tore it to pieces.
34. Mr. Briggs, a lawyer from London, objected on the grounds that Mr. Rochester was already married.
35. He wanted to show them Bertha, his insane wife, so they would understand why he wanted to marry Jane and have a normal relationship.
36. His father and her family pushed the marriage on him; Bertha was beautiful so he cooperated. Later, he learned that insanity ran in her family.
37. Mr. Mason is acquainted with Jane's uncle, and Jane had written to him telling him about her marriage to Mr. Rochester.
38. run away together, spend their lives traveling over the continent
39. The next morning Jane got on a coach to Whitcross.
40. a light
41. The sisters were kind and concerned; St. John was rather cold.
42. teaching the local children
43. They will not inherit his fortune.
44. the daughter of the only rich man in St. John's parish; St. John secretly loves her.
45. He saw Jane's real name, "Eyre" scribbled on the edge of a piece of paper. His Uncle John's name was Eyre. He made inquiries and made the connection.
46. She inherited Uncle John's fortune; she split it with the Rivers.
47. They are her cousins.
48. Christmas
49. He wanted her to learn Hindustani with him and go to India as his wife/missionary.
50. She did not love him.
51. He was very cold and acted as though she were shunning her Christian duty.
52. She thought she heard his voice calling her.
53. Bertha set it on fire, then dove into the flames herself.
54. He was trying to save Bertha from the fire.
55. He was at Ferndean, and delighted to hear her voice and hold her.
56. Jane and Mr. Rochester married and began a family. They are very happy. Adèle finished school and is now a dear companion of Jane's. St. John is still in India, near death.
57. Some possible themes: early feminism; questioning of religion; nature of true love; the "rightness" of honesty, integrity, forgiveness, courage, family love; the silliness of social classes and superficial behavior.
58. Students' answers will vary.

Activity #2: Sample map:

Synonyms:		Antonyms:
fierce		gentle
hostile	**TRUCULENT**	amiable
belligerent		
rotten and nasty		

Sentence: The boy's truculent behavior was a mystery to his teacher, who couldn't understand why he was so angry.

Visual or memory device: angry-looking face

Activity #3: 1-chilblains; 2-cuirass; 3-moiety; 4-surtout; 5-soporific; 6-10 will vary. 11-porte cochère (covered carriage entrance); the others all describe clothes that protect the body; 12-confabulation (chatting); the others all have to do with the face and interpreting its expressions; 13-dissipations (dissolute amusements, as by excess drinking); the others are all pieces of furniture; 14-malevolent (spiteful); the others all have to do with inconsistency, but not deliberate hurtfulness; 15-raiment (clothing); the others are all types of people; 16-salubrious (healthful); the others all have to do with optimism/pessimism

Activity #4: 1-anathematized; 2-propitious; 3-exonerated; 4-acrimony; 5-saturnine; 6-extirpate; 7-contumacy; 8-sonorous; 9-sagacity; 10-protracted; 11-predecessor; 12-sordid; 13-meretricious; 14-phlegmatic

Activity #5: (sample answers) 1-No, an ostler (or hostler; one who takes care of horses) has legs. 2-Yes, a magic potion is often a liquid. 3-Yes, someone might steal a letter. 4-No, your mien is your appearance or bearing, not a container. 5-No, an infant isn't old enough to be interested in finances. 6-Yes, you should mistrust a quack. 7-No, a fish doesn't have an intellect. 8-Yes, you usually are happy when your parents approve of what you want to do. 9-Yes, you might find eggs in an eagle's nest. 10-Yes, a beautiful woman can be a source of attraction.

Activity #6: 1-buffoon; 2-moneylender; 3-accorded; 4-mystery; 5-irritable; 6-teasing; 7-harem; 8-intensify; 9-childish; 10-humble

Activity #7: 1-plover; 2-superfluous; 3-remuneration; 4-chimera; 5-aperture; 6-prurience; 7-debauchery; 8-eschewed; 9-interlocutor; 10-profligate; 11-unalloyed

Activity #8: 1-morass; 2-boon; 3-inducements; 4-immutably; 5-halcyon; 6-ignoble; 7-sloth; 8-assiduous; 9-asp; 10-zealous; 11-testily; 12-coruscating; 13-hiatus; 14-recrimination; 15-hoary

Activity #9: (sample answers) 1-bubbling, simmering; 2-attainment, success; 3-separation, rebuffing; 4-talkative, verbose; 5-compact, seminal; 6-esteemed, revered; 7-metaphysical, mystical; 8-manacles, shackles; 9-reliable, unerring; 10-karma, kismet; 11-cash, dollars; 12-alms, dole; 13-becalm, conciliate

There are no specific answers for the remaining open-ended activities.

Comprehension Quiz—Short Answer: (Answers may vary somewhat.)
1-Mrs. Reed had promised her husband, Jane's uncle, that she would raise the orphaned girl. 2-Mrs. Reed never liked Jane, and after Jane fought back against John's bullying, she decided to get Jane out of her hair. 3-Mr. Brocklehurst told the girls and teachers to avoid Jane because she was deceitful and bad. 4-Miss Temple was a gentle, pious teacher whom Jane loved. 5-Helen was a gentle, bright girl who died of consumption. 6-Seven years earlier, Uncle John had visited Mrs. Reed in search of his niece, Jane. 7-She decided that she wanted to experience more of the world. 8-Mrs. Fairfax's employer, Mr. Rochester, needed a tutor for his charge, Adèle. 9-She let him lean on her shoulder after he hurt himself in a fall from his horse. 10-She doused him with water and wakened him. 11-drawing 12-to bring home guests 13-gypsy 14-ring 15-aloof and disturbed 16-Grace Poole 17-Adèle 18-porter/alcoholic drink 19-resemble 20-singing voice

Comprehension Quiz—Objective: 1-T; 2-F; 3-T; 4-F; 5-F; 6-T; 7-T; 8-F; 9-T; 10-F; 11-F; 12-F; 13-T; 14-F; 15-F; 16-F; 17-T; 18-T; 19-T; 20-T

Unit Exam—Honors Level:
Identification: A-6; B-11; C-8; D-21; E-7; F-13; G-2; H-20; I-12; J-10; K-3; L-17; M-5; N-19; 0-1; P-9; Q-15; R-18; S-16; T-14; U-4; V-23; W-22

Multiple Choice: 1-2; 2-3; 3-2; 4-2; 5-1; 6-3; 7-4; 8-3; 9-4; 10-3; 11-1; 12-2; 13-3; 14-3; 15-4; 16-3; 17-1; 18-4; 19-2; 20-1; 21-2; 22-1; 23-4; 24-1; 25-4; 26-3; 27-3; 28-1; 29-4; 30-4

Analysis:
A. Students who choose (1) may defend the idea that Jane left Mr. Rochester because she could not have lived with herself, otherwise. Students who choose (2) may defend the idea that Jane has been "brainwashed" to believe that staying with Mr. Rochester is morally wrong, although her heart tells her otherwise.
B. Students who choose (1) might point out that Jane seems happy at the end, living with Mr. Rochester and raising their family. Students who choose (2) might point out that Jane is a talented artist and avid reader who would enjoy illustrating books. Students who choose (3) might point to the many passages in which Jane pleads for the rights of women. Students who choose (4) might mention that Jane has had quite a bit of teaching experience at Lowood and as Adèle's governess.

Critical/Creative Thinking:
C. The diary should contain the insight that the Rivers are the counterparts of the Reeds—truly the "family" that the Reeds might have been, but failed to be.
D. The tree is split by lightning the night before Mr. Rochester and Jane were to be "joined" in marriage—but were instead torn apart. Like the two portions of the tree, each survived on his/her own, but a less satisfying existence than when united.

Unit Exam—Average Level:
Identification: A-6; B-11; C-8; D-21; E-7; F-13; G-2; H-20; I-12; J-10; K-3; L-17; M-5; N-19; 0-1; P-9; Q-15; R-18; S-16; T-14; U-4; V-23; W-22

Multiple Choice: 1-4; 2-4; 3-2; 4-1; 5-3; 6-4; 7-1; 8-3; 9-3; 10-3; 11-1; 12-3; 13-3; 14-1; 15-1; 16-3; 17-3; 18-4; 19-2; 20-2; 21-3; 22-2; 23-2; 24-4; 25-2; 26-4; 27-1; 28-4; 29-4; 30-1

Analysis:
A. Students should explain that she hears Mr. Rochester's voice, realizes she still loves him, that he needs her, and that she doesn't belong with St. John.
B. Students might analyze some of the dreams about infants that seem to indicate Jane's loss of control and her fear of losing the ones she loves.

Critical/Creative Thinking:
C. The letter might describe Adèle's giddiness, Mrs. Fairfax's kindness, and Mr. Rochester's gruffness. Jane might make a subtle allusion to her romantic interest in her employer.
D. There is evidence in the novel that Jane would stay with Mr. Rochester—even if his wife were still around.